GEOGRAPHY AND HISTORY
SECONDARY

BY ME

Cristina Granda Gallego
Raúl Núñez Heras
Simon Baskett
Tim Bacon

ANCIENT GREECE

Contents

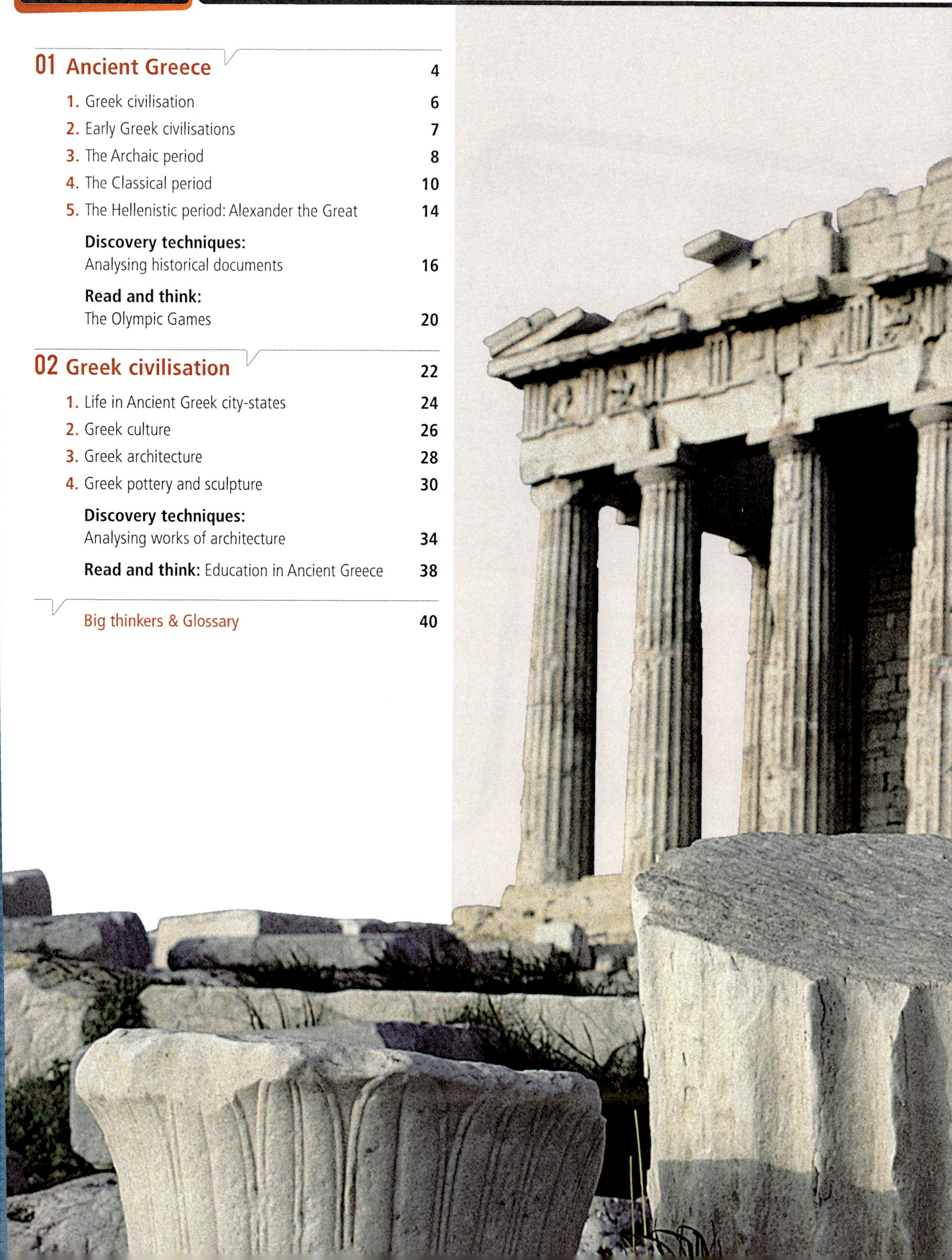

01 Ancient Greece

<< LOOKING BACK

- Name the capital city of modern-day Greece.
- Can you name the international sporting event that originated in Ancient Greece?
- Can you name an Ancient Greek colony on the Iberian Peninsula?
- What art form are the Ancient Greeks best known for?
- What takes place in the buildings in pictures B and D?
- Look at pictures A–D. How do you think Ancient Greek civilisation has influenced modern civilisation?

A The ruins of the stadium at Delphi, central Greece

B The Olympic Stadium in Barcelona

C The ruins of the *Ecclesia* (public assembly) at Messene, souther[n] Greece

Sparta: a military state

Imagine a place where all the people are trained to fight and be fierce, physically fit and totally obedient. You might be thinking of Nazi Germany or Fascist Italy... But, in fact, the first military state was the Ancient Greek city-state of Sparta.

At the age of seven, Spartan boys left home and went to military school. There they had to fight, undergo tough physical tests and learn survival skills, such as stealing food and walking barefoot in cold weather. At the age of 20, Spartan men became soldiers and were expected to serve in the army until the age of 60.

Spartan women were given more freedom than women in other parts of Ancient Greece, but were expected to have lots of children (preferably boys). All newborn babies were brought before a council which examined them for physical defects. If a baby was considered too weak, it would be left outside to die.

It is not surprising that the Spartans were feared warriors and that they dominated Greece for some time. However, they were eventually defeated by their rival city-state of Thebes.

- What is your opinion of Spartan society? And of Spartan education?
- Do you think there still are military states today? Do you think military service is a good thing?

D

The European Parliament in Strasbourg

LOOKING FORWARD >>

- What was the terrain of Ancient Greece like?
- Where was the Minoan civilisation located?
- Where did the first Ancient Greek city-state emerge?
- What was an Ancient Greek infantry soldier called?
- How old was Alexander the Great when he died?

1 Greek civilisation

What was the terrain of Ancient Greece like?

1.1 Geographical factors

Ancient Greek civilisation began in the **west of the Mediterranean**, between the Ionian Sea and the Aegean Sea. The territory of this civilisation covered the south of the Balkan Peninsula and archipelagos such as the Cyclades islands. The Ancient Greeks referred to this area as **Hellas**. Over time, Greek civilisation expanded its territory into new areas through colonisation.

The **terrain of Hellas was mountainous** and largely formed of narrow valleys surrounded by steep mountains. This mountainous terrain influenced the way this civilisation developed in a number of ways:

- **It was difficult to travel** from one settlement to another. It was often easier to travel by sea. The Ancient Greeks were very good sailors.
- As there were not many large plains or rivers, the terrain was not very suitable for agriculture. This meant that people had to **trade** more.
- The terrain did not favour the development of large kingdoms. This meant that small **city-states**, known as **poleis**, formed.

HELLAS AND HELLENISM

Hellas is the term we use to describe the geographical area of Ancient Greece. It is also the origin of some other terms. A *Hellene* refers to an inhabitant of Hellas. The term *Hellenic* is a synonym for *Greek*, i.e. when we say Hellenic art, we could also say Ancient Greek art.

1.2 A different type of civilisation

Even though Ancient Greece was made up of many different city-states, the Greeks **were aware of their own collective personality**. They shared a common language, culture and other social characteristics which differentiated them from other ancient civilisations.

Unlike the Ancient Egyptians and Mesopotamians, whose gods were distant and all-powerful, the Greeks believed their gods were like humans in appearance and in the way they thought. Similarly, priests did not have as much power in Greece. Greek culture was more concerned with the human being. Their way of thinking was rational and critical. This is why philosophy developed greatly in Greece during this period.

ACTIVITIES

1. Explain how Ancient Greece was different from other ancient civilisations, such as Egypt and Mesopotamia.
2. Name one characteristic that Ancient Greece had in common with the Sumerian civilisation.
3. Look at the map above. Then, use an atlas or an online map to find out which modern-day countries are located in the territory shown.

2 Early Greek civilisations

Where was the Minoan civilisation located?

Ancient Greek civilisation was preceded by two other civilisations: the **Minoan civilisation**, on the island of Crete, and the **Mycenaean civilisation**, in the north-east of the Peloponnese peninsula.

2.1 Minoan civilisation

Crete is the most fertile island in the Aegean Sea. Agriculture began to develop here around 7000 BC. Because of its location on **trade routes** between Africa, Asia and Europe, **craftwork** developed, as did a large fleet of merchant ships and war ships. This **economic development** led to the emergence of the Minoan civilisation.

We have evidence of the Minoan civilisation from about 2600 BC. The ruins of its cities suggest that it had a high **standard of living**. In **cities** such as Knossos (the capital of Minoan civilisation) and Phaistos, the palace was the centre of power.

By the middle of the 15th century BC (around 1450 BC), the Minoan culture had been destroyed by conquerors from mainland Greece.

The Palace of Knossos was the most important in all of Crete and its king was probably the most powerful ruler on the island. The walls of this palace were decorated with colourful frescoes.

A reconstructed bull-leaping fresco in the Palace of Knossos

2.2 A different type of civilisation

The **Mycenaean civilisation** emerged on the Peloponnese peninsula on mainland Greece between 1700 and 1500 BC. This civilisation was divided into **small kingdoms** ruled by kings. Under these kings there was a powerful military **aristocracy** and, below them, a base of farm labourers.

Mycenaean palaces were royal residences. They were protected by massive walls. The most important palace was in **Mycenae**.

The Lion Gate in Mycenae

The Mycenaean civilisation experienced a crisis between the years 1200 and 1150 BC which marked the beginning of its decline. Following its decline, Greece entered a **Dark Age**.

ACTIVITIES

4. Find Crete and the Peloponnese peninsula on the map on the previous page.
5. Why was Crete such a good location for economic development?
6. Do these two early Greek civilisations correspond to Prehistory or to Ancient History?

3 The Archaic period

➲ Where did the first Ancient Greek city-state emerge?

After the fall of Mycenae, Greece entered a **Dark Age**, lasting from about 1200 BC to 800 BC. This period was characterised by economic decline and migration to Ionia, on the coast of Anatolia. Ionia was extremely important because it was where the first **Greek polis**, or **city-state**, emerged in the course of the 9th century BC, during the Dark Age. It became the model for political organisation in Greece.

3.1 The emergence of poleis

There were several hundred poleis in Greece, most of which developed during the Archaic period (*c.* 800–480 BC). At the beginning of the Archaic period, the poleis were governed by a **military aristocracy**, which owned large areas of land. Below this aristocracy were peasants, artisans and slaves.

The shortage of arable land and the aristocracy's monopoly over it meant that **social conflict** was common. Many peasants became enslaved because of large debts they owed to the landowners.

THE STRUCTURE OF A POLIS

A polis was made up of two main areas:

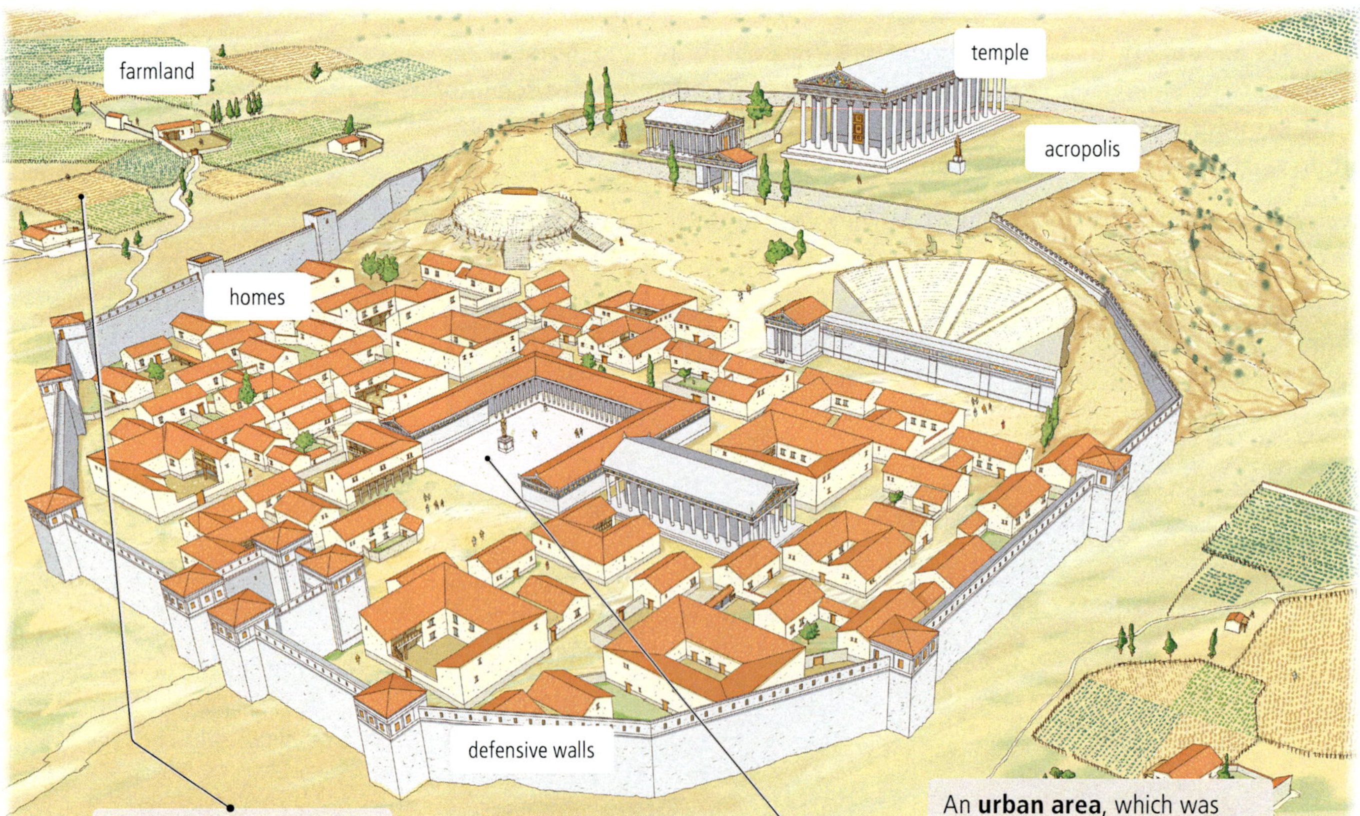

A **dependent territory,** located outside the city walls, which was used for farming.

An **urban area**, which was usually protected by defensive walls. The acropolis was an elevated part of the urban area where the most important buildings were located.

3.2 Territorial expansion: colonisation

One of the most important phenomena of the Archaic period was **colonisation**: a process by which Greek settlements **were established** throughout the Mediterranean.

The first colonies were established in the south of modern-day Italy and on the island of Sicily, an area known as **Magna Graecia**. Later, they founded colonies along the Mediterranean coast and around the Black Sea.

Colonisation was the **response** of aristocratic governments **to social instability**. However, the social problems continued because a **minority still possessed most of the land** and it was still not distributed evenly.

As a result of colonisation:

- **Trade** was stimulated and merchants grew rich and powerful.
- Greek city-states became the greatest **maritime powers** in the Mediterranean until the 6th century BC.
- Colonies were set up by colonisers from Greek city-states. The colonisers helped spread Greek culture, a phenomenon known as **Hellenisation**.

TYRANNY AND TYRANTS

As the merchants became rich from colonisation, they wanted more involvement in government, but the aristocracy refused.

In many city-states, the **merchants** formed alliances with the **leaders of the armies**, which were made up of peasants and craftsmen. They overthrew the aristocracy and established **tyrannies**, which were authoritarian governments led by one person, known as a **tyrant**.

These governments implemented **authoritarian social reforms**, dividing the land amongst the peasants. So, the aristocracy lost its privileges and its power.

GREEK COLONISATION

ACTIVITIES

7. Write definitions for the following terms: *polis*, *acropolis*, *tyrant*, *Hellenisation*.

8. Explain why colonisation did not provide a solution for social instability. What were the consequences of Greek colonisation?

9. Find and identify the Greek colonies on the Iberian Peninsula. Find out what their modern-day names are.

4 The Classical period

What was an Ancient Greek infantry soldier called?

The Classical period refers to the period between the **Greco-Persian Wars**, at the beginning of the 5th century BC, and the **death of Alexander the Great** in 323 BC. This period was characterised by wars and conflicts, but it was also the greatest period of social and cultural achievement in Ancient Greece.

Infantry soldiers in Ancient Greek armies were called *hoplites*. They fought in a close formation called a *phalanx*.

4.1 The Greco-Persian Wars

The **Persian Empire**, which already occupied the Near East, Ionia and Thrace, tried to gain control of Greece, starting in the 5th century BC. A **coalition of Greek cities** fought the Persian forces in a conflict known as the Greco-Persian Wars, which took place between 490 and 480–479 BC. At the **battles of Marathon and Salamis**, the Greek armies defeated the powerful Persian forces.

A relief sculpture of Greek soldiers in battle with the Persians

Greece's victory over the Persians liberated city-states which had been conquered, reinforced common Greek values in all city-states and strengthened the leadership of the city-states of **Athens** and **Sparta**.

After serving as leaders in the Greco-Persian Wars, Athens and Sparta became rivals, forming leagues **of cities** around them. These leagues were alliances created for political and military purposes.

ACTIVITIES

10. When did the Classical period begin and end?
11. How did the Greeks' victory over the Persians affect their city-states?
12. Find out why many historians believe that hoplites were the best soldiers in the Ancient Mediterranean World.

4.2 Athens

After the Greco-Persian Wars, Athens achieved a dominant position in Ancient Greece through **hegemony**:

- It was the leader of the **Delian League**, over which it exercised full control.
- The city-states that were members of the Delian League all shared a common system of government, called **democracy**. The basis of democracy was the participation of citizens in government. This political system came into existence following the overthrow of the aristocracy by some social groups during the Archaic period.
- Athens developed a **trade-based economy**, which was the most prosperous in Ancient Greece. Because of the superiority of the Athenian navy and its control over the cities in the Delian League, Athens was an **important centre of maritime trade**.

PERICLES

Athenian democracy was the result of the collective effort of the Athenian people and figures like Pericles. He was a magistrate who strengthened democracy and led Athens to its period of greatest glory.

Pericles did this by making the *Ecclesia* more important, implementing policies for the protection of citizens and turning Athens into a beautiful city. Because of his efforts, the Athenians granted him the title of 'first citizen'.

THE ACROPOLIS OF ATHENS

During the Greco-Persian Wars, the Athenian acropolis was destroyed by the Persians. Pericles encouraged the city to rebuild the acropolis, using the resources of the Delian League. The acropolis was a religious space dedicated to the city's protector, the goddess Athena. It was the site of some of the greatest works of art in **antiquity**.

The Parthenon temple

The Porch of the Caryatids

The Acropolis complex seen from a distance

ACTIVITIES

13. How did Athens achieve a dominant position following the Greco-Persian Wars?

14. Why was Athens such an important maritime-trading city?

15. Find out which Greek city-states were members of the Delian League.

Athenian democracy

The **egalitarian** reforms of the Athenian tyrants contributed to the development of **Athenian democracy**, which was based on:

- **Obedience** of the law.
- **Citizenship**: Being a citizen meant having political rights and obligations, as well as taking part in government.

Athenian citizens participated directly in government through institutions, such as the main **assembly** (***Ecclesia***) and the ***Boule***, a council made up of 500 citizens:

Citizens

participated in the

***Ecclesia* (assembly)**

Every citizen had the right to speak and vote in the *Ecclesia*. Here, laws were passed and decisions on foreign policy were made. The decisions proposed by the *Boule* were also decided on.

participated voluntarily in the

***Heliaia* (supreme court)**

Here citizens were judged, although no judges, lawyers or civil servants worked there.

drew lots to appoint the

***Boule* (council of the 500)**

The *Boule* wrote laws and prepared policies which were debated in the *Ecclesia*.

controlled the

annually elected the

Magistrates

Magistrates were government officials who enforced the laws made by the *Boule*.

of which there were two main types

Strategoi

These magistrates were military generals who were in charge of the army.

Archons

A group of nine chief magistrates, who were in charge of the civil service.

A limited democracy

Only a **minority of Athenians were citizens**, i.e. free men who were all born in Athens. Women, foreigners and slaves were excluded from citizenship. Because citizenship did not include all the inhabitants of Athens, Athenian democracy is considered a **limited democracy**.

THE DEVELOPMENT OF POLITICAL SYSTEMS IN ANCIENT GREECE

Aristocracy

Government made up of a small group of nobles and landowners.

↓

Tyranny

Authoritarian government led by one person, known as a tyrant.

↓

Democracy

Political system in which citizens are involved in making decisions.

BIG THINKER

Cleisthenes was an Athenian noble who changed the voting system in the city-state so poor citizens could have an equal say in government. The system was called *democracy*, meaning 'power of the people'. Cleisthenes reduced the power of the aristocratic families and to stop one person gaining too much power, he introduced the practice of 'ostracism'. This practice involved people scratching the name of the most unpopular man in Athens on a piece of clay. The 'winner' would be **banished** from the city for 10 years.

Do you think ostracism happens on reality television?

4.3 Sparta

The city of Sparta was a military power and the leader of the **Peloponnesian League**, which was made up of cities that opposed Athenian dominance.

Sparta had an **aristocratic government** known as a **diarchy**, because it was led by two kings. Spartan kings came from the aristocracy, which controlled power through the **Council of Elders**, or ***Gerousia***.

The Spartan economy was based on **agriculture**. The hardest labour was done by ***helots,*** who were state-owned slaves. Most of the population were ***perioeci,*** which were farmers and artisans with military obligations but no political rights.

4.4 The Peloponnesian War

Between 431 and 404 BC, **Athens and Sparta**, together with their respective leagues, fought in the Peloponnesian War. **Sparta won.**

This war weakened all Greek cities and led to social and economic **decline**. Despite its victory, not long afterwards, Sparta was forced to give way to the leadership of **Thebes**, and later, to kingdoms such as **Macedonia**.

SPARTAN WARRIORS

The concept of citizenship that existed in Athens did not exist in Sparta. Its citizens, known as Spartiates, were free and had rights, but above all they were soldiers.

All Spartan citizens were full-time soldiers and they spent their lives training for battle. Therefore, Spartan citizens lived in **harsh** conditions and resided in military **quarters** from childhood. Physical fitness was very important to them, as they had to be prepared for battle at all times.

DID YOU KNOW?

Spartan women had their hair cut very short when preparing for marriage and kept their hair short afterwards. Married couples often lived apart because men under the age of 30 had to live with other soldiers in military quarters, although they sometimes escaped to spend time with their wives. Spartan women were encouraged to have lots of children and were rewarded if they produced boys to fight in the army.

Do you think women were treated fairly in Spartan society?

ACTIVITIES

16. Study the map on this page. Which league was the greatest maritime power? Which was the least powerful? Explain how this is related to the main economic activities of the two city-states that led the leagues.

17. What differentiates Ancient Greek democracy from the main forms of government in other early civilisations?

18. Compare the consequences of the Greco-Persian Wars and the Peloponnesian War. What was the difference between the two wars?

5 The Hellenistic period: Alexander the Great

How old was Alexander the Great when he died?

5.1 Macedonian dominance

Macedonia was a kingdom located to the north of Greece. It was **culturally different** from Classical Greece and the Greeks considered it barbarian, i.e. a non-Greek kingdom. The king of Macedonia, **Philip II**, helped spread Greek culture throughout Macedonia. In 338 BC, he defeated a league of Greek city-states that united against him at Chaeronea.

In 337 BC Philip II established the **League of Corinth**. It united all of the cities of Greece, except for Sparta, under Macedonian control. When Philip II died in 336 BC, his son **Alexander the Great** became king and consolidated Macedonian control over Greece.

5.2 The empire of Alexander the Great

Alexander the Great was only 20 years old when he became king of Macedonia. He was a cultured man, educated by the most important intellectual of the period, the philosopher **Aristotle**. He was very **skilled in politics and war**. Over a period of 13 years, he made many **conquests**, forming an **empire** that **united East and West**. His aim was to build a **world empire** through:

- **Military conquests**, which enabled him to take control of vast territories where Greek, Egyptian, Mesopotamian and Persian civilisations had been established, reaching as far as India.
- Implementing a centralised political system. This system already existed in Persia and Alexander used it in order to have absolute power.
- Surrounding himself with a complex court for ceremonies, as Alexander was also considered as a god.
- Promoting **trade** in his empire by introducing a **single currency**.
- Supporting the **spread** of **Greek culture** into the East. He founded new cities and made **Greek the official language** of the empire.

ALEXANDER THE GREAT

The life of Alexander the Great has been recorded by many ancient historians. However, their accounts of him often differ greatly:

"The love for Philosophy that Aristotle gave to Alexander never left his soul. [...] In general, Alexander was arrogant towards the peoples of the East. He was convinced of his own divine origins. With the Greeks, however, Alexander was more cautious of describing himself as a god."

PLUTARCH, *Parallel Lives* (Adapted)

"In the middle of a celebration, Alexander stabbed and killed Cleitus, who was a childhood friend of Alexander's. Cleitus was reluctant to worship Alexander. He was also reluctant to transform himself from a Macedonian free man into a Persian slave."

SENECA, *On Anger* (Adapted)

ACTIVITIES

19. Read the two texts about Alexander the Great again and answer the following questions:

a. Which aspects of Alexander's conquests are mentioned in each text?
b. Each text mentions a different aspect of Alexander's personality. Write two adjectives that you think can be applied to Alexander in each case.
c. In groups, find out who the authors of the texts were; where they were from; and when they lived.
d. Then, discuss why you think the two descriptions of Alexander are different.

5.3 The Hellenistic kingdoms

The premature death of Alexander the Great in 323 BC at the age of 33, before he had named a successor, caused **his empire to break up** into a number of kingdoms known as the **Hellenistic kingdoms**.

The most important of these kingdoms were Macedonia, Pergamon, Egypt and the Seleucid Empire. Alexander's plan for a world empire was lost when these kingdoms formed, but many of the policies implemented by him continued:

- **Trade** received a powerful boost, spreading to China, Arabia and Central Asia.
- There was **intensive urban development**. Greek cities were overtaken in importance by places like Ephesus, Alexandria, Pergamon and Rhodes.
- Hellenistic **culture** spread and merged with Eastern cultures. Later, Rome assimilated Hellenistic culture as well.

HELLENISM AND HELLENIC

The term *Hellenistic*, which refers to the kingdoms that succeeded Alexander the Great following his death, should not be confused with the word *Hellenic*, which is a synonym for *Greek*.

THE EMPIRE OF ALEXANDER THE GREAT

ACTIVITIES

20. What did the word *barbarian* mean to the Greeks?

21. How did Alexander the Great aim to build a world empire?

22. Study the map on this page and name cities founded by Alexander the Great. Do you notice anything unusual about them? What do you think is the connection between this and how his empire was organised?

23. Answer the questions.

a. What was the name of the league established by Philip II?

b. Who educated Alexander the Great?

c. What happened to Alexander's empire following his death?

Discovery techniques

ANALYSING HISTORICAL DOCUMENTS

A historical document is a **written text** from the past. Historical documents are essential to the work of historians. In order to analyse a historical document, we must follow the same steps as we would with any text.

1. Careful reading of a text

First, you should **read** the text carefully several times and underline or make notes about the main ideas, names, dates and information.

2. Context

Next, you need to put the document into context. That means you must describe the **external aspects** of the text, such as the **author**, the **type of document** and the **historical background**. You can research this in books or on the internet.

	EXTERNAL ASPECTS
Author	If the author is known, you should include a brief description of him or her.
Type of document	Historical documents can be public (laws, speeches, books, etc.) or private (letters, private diaries, etc.).
Historical background	You should describe when and where the events mentioned in the document took place, i.e. what year or years they took place in, and the period of History.

3. Analysis

In your analysis, you must identify the **main ideas** of the text. Then, you need to organise these ideas to identify the **main idea** and any **secondary ideas** that may serve to support the main idea.

4. Commentary

In this section, you should explain your ideas, supporting them with the historical aspects that appear in the text. You should not mention points which are not related to the **subject matter**, nor give an opinion about the document. To write this section:

a) Prepare an outline to help you organise your ideas.

b) Using this outline, begin to write your commentary, explaining what you know about the historical period and relating this to the information in the text.

c) Do not simply copy the original text. Use your own words!

5. Assessment or critique

Finally, you should explain aspects which are not specifically mentioned in the text, but which you can deduce from it.

To do this you should ask yourself questions, such as:

- How does the author feel about what they are writing?
- Are they in favour of it or against it?
- Why are they writing what they are writing? What is their motivation?
- What don't they say in the text?
- What arguments do they use?

As a conclusion, you should summarise the ideas you have written in your assessment. This will make it easier for the reader to understand them.

On the next page, you are going to read a historical document. Then, you will see an example of how to analyse it. Only the first three steps are done. You will have to do the rest yourself.

Pericles' Funeral Oration

"Our constitution does not copy the laws of neighbouring city-states; we are more a model for others than imitators ourselves. Our administration favours the many instead of the few; this is why it is called a democracy. We open our city-state to the world, and never deny foreigners the opportunity of observing or learning from us.

In education, where our rivals give great importance to manliness from the day they are born through painful discipline, in Athens we live exactly as we please. However, we are just as ready to go into battle when necessary.

The elegance of our buildings and structures is a daily source of pleasure for our citizens and helps to eliminate boredom; while the greatness of our city attracts goods from all over the world into our harbour."

THUCYDIDES, *The History of the Peloponnesian War*
Fordham University (Adapted)

A bust of Pericles

1. Careful reading of a text

After reading the whole text once, read it again and make notes.

2. Context

	EXTERNAL ASPECTS
Author	Thucydides, an Athenian historian who lived from 465–395 BC.
Type of document	The text is a public document. It is an extract from a history book that would have been publicly available. It also contains a speech made in public by Pericles.
Historical background	The text was written in the late 5th century BC, as Athens began to decline as a result of its war with Sparta.

3. Analysis

Main idea: Athens is a model for Greece because it is superior to other Greek city-states.

Secondary ideas which support the main idea:

- Political and social superiority due to its democratic system and attitude towards foreigners.
- Military superiority, because its inhabitants defend the city because of a sense of civic duty.
- Artistic superiority because of its buildings and structures.
- Economic superiority due to it being a centre of trade.

ACTIVITIES

1. Write the commentary and assessment for the text by Thucydides, following the steps on the previous page. In your commentary, you should mention: the economy, society and democratic system of Athens; how Athens and Sparta differed; and Athenian art and architecture.
2. In ancient Athens, were foreigners treated as fairly as Thucydides says? Explain your answer.
3. Analyse this historical text:

"The basis of a democratic state is liberty. In a democracy, the majority must be hold power, and whatever the majority approve should be considered just.

Every citizen, it is said, must have equality, and therefore in a democracy, the poor have more power than the rich, because there are more of them, and the opinion of the majority is what counts. This is one of the most distinctive aspects of freedom, an aspect which all democrats consider a defining element of their state.

Another characteristic is that a man should live as he likes. This, they say, is the privilege of a free man, since not to live as a man likes is the mark of a slave."

ARISTOTLE, *Politics*
Fordham University (Adapted)

Revision activities

1. How did the natural environment of Greece influence the development of Ancient Greek civilisation? Mention at least two factors.

2. Create a guide to one of these two sites: the Palace of Knossos or Mycenae. Choose one of them and write a pamphlet giving information about: location, date or period, how to get there, history of the site and what you can see there.

3. Make a timeline of Ancient Greek civilisation. Your timeline should be divided into four main sections, one for each period of Ancient Greek civilisation (Early civilisations, Archaic, Classical and Hellenistic). Then, place the following events in the correct period and order. Include dates for the beginning and end of events when appropriate:

- Macedonian dominance
- Emergence of poleis
- Greco-Persian Wars
- Battle of Marathon
- Colonisation
- Minoan civilisation
- The Peloponnesian War
- Alexander the Great
- League of Corinth
- Philip II
- Hellenistic kingdoms
- Battle of Salamis
- Mycenaean civilisation

4. Define the following terms: *Hellas, colonisation, Hellenistic kingdoms, Hellenism, Hellenisation, Minoan civilisation, Mycenaean civilisation, tyrant, Magna Graecia, Ecclesia, diarchy, polis, acropolis.*

5. What exactly do we mean when we say that democracy in Athens was a 'limited democracy'?

6. Imagine you are in the agora of an Ancient Greek polis. You are going to hold a class debate. Get into two groups. One group is going to defend the Athenian political system of Pericles. The other group is going to defend the Spartan political system. Each group must first research their political system and prepare arguments to defend it.

7. Look the picture below. It is a coin showing the head of Alexander the Great with the horns of the Egyptian god Amun. What policies implemented by Alexander are reflected in the picture? You should be able to name two policies. Look closely at Alexander's head!

8. Compare democracy in ancient Athens with democracy in Spain today. Which do you think is more democratic? Justify your answer. Use the following questions to help you:
   - Who was able to vote in Athens? Who can vote in Spain today?
   - Why do you think certain people could not vote in Athens? Do you think this was fair or unfair? Why?
   - Could children vote in Athens? Can they in Spain? Would you like to be allowed to vote? Why?

9. Compare Athens and Sparta. Copy and complete this table in your notebook.

	ATHENS	SPARTA
Political system		
Economy		
Citizens		
League		

10. Decide if the following statements are causes or consequences of Ancient Greek colonisation:
    a. Trade was stimulated and merchants grew rich.
    b. Greek city-states became the greatest maritime powers in the Mediterranean until the 6th century BC.
    c. Farmland was not distributed evenly.
    d. Greek settlements were established throughout the Mediterranean.
    e. Greek culture spread throughout the Mediterranean, a phenomenon known as Hellenisation.

11. Select your favourite of the following quotes attributed to Pericles. Explain why you chose it.
    - 'Freedom is the only possession of those who have the courage to defend it.'
    - 'Just because you do not take an interest in politics doesn't mean that politics won't take an interest in you.'
    - 'Time is the king of all men. He is their parent and their grave, and gives them what he wants and not what they want.'

12. Briefly explain why these figures were important: Pericles, Philip II, Alexander the Great.

13. Define Hellenistic culture. Then, explain how Alexander the Great helped to spread it.

14 Describe the political system implemented by Alexander the Great in the territories he conquered. How did this system differ from Athenian democracy?

15 Think and assess. Was Alexander the Great a great ruler?

- Work with a partner. Discuss the qualities a great ruler should have and write them down in your notebook.
- Read about how Alexander the Great built his empire on page 14.
- Now write your assessment: Was Alexander a great ruler? Why or why not? Give reasons for your answer.

16 Use the map of the empire of Alexander the Great on page 15 and an atlas, or an online map, to name the modern-day countries which were once part of the empire.

17 Copy and complete the following table:

	GRECO-PERSIAN WARS	PELOPONNESIAN WAR
Dates		
Who fought		
Main battles		
Who won		

18 These two statues come from Sparta. Read the texts about Sparta on pages 5 and 13, and explain how they represent Spartan education and the Spartan warrior mentality.

19 Copy or trace the map below in your notebook and do the following activities:

a. Mark the territory of Hellas.

b. Use colours to represent the areas colonised in Ionia, the Mediterranean and the Black Sea.

c. Mark at least two colonies in each of the colonised areas.

d. Find out which modern-day countries are located in the territories colonised by the Greeks.

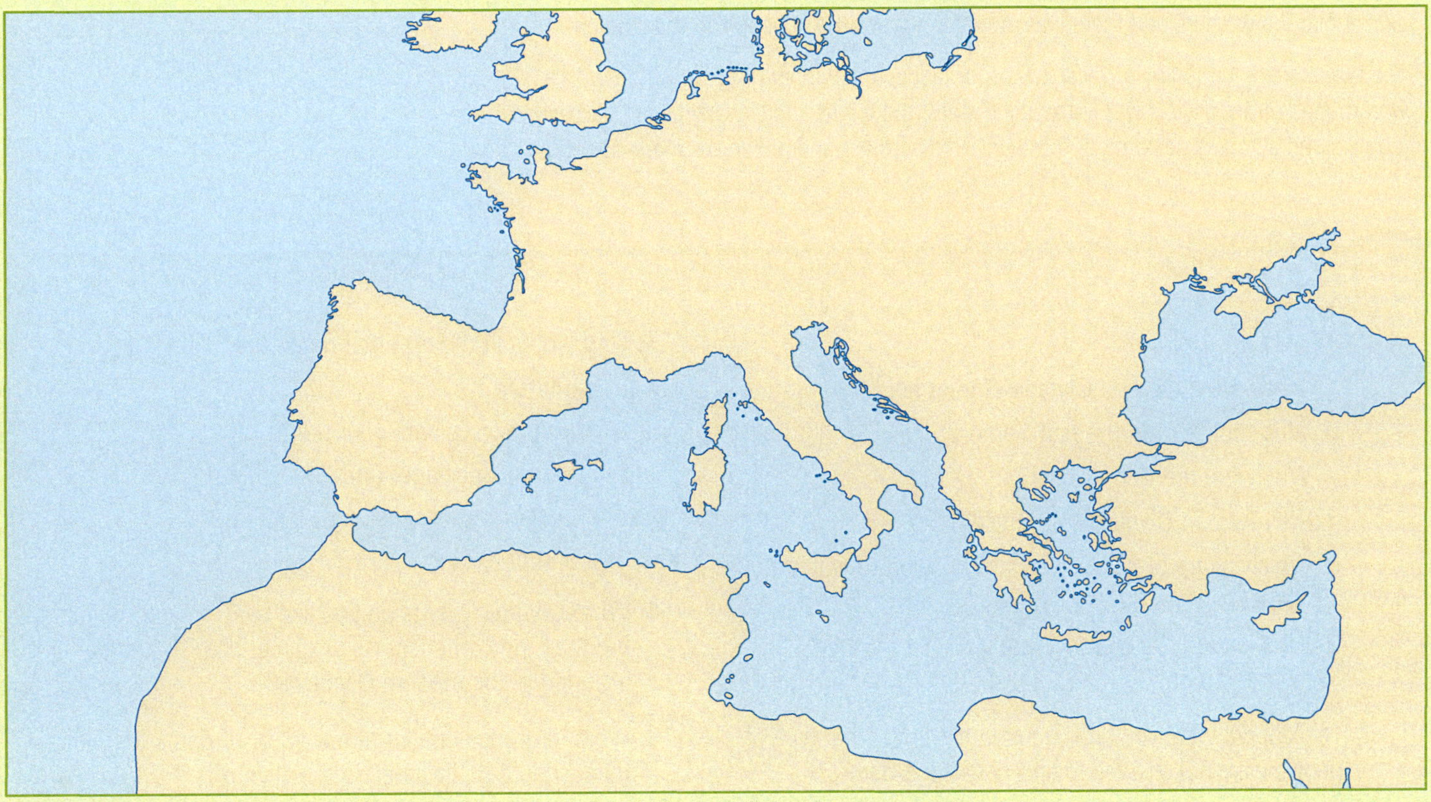

Read and think

THE OLYMPIC GAMES

Our modern Olympic Games only started at the end of the 19th century. In our modern games, men and women from all round the world compete in over thirty Olympic events at games which last for about two weeks.

The first Olympic Games were held in Olympia in south-west Greece in about 776 BC. Only free men who spoke Greek were allowed to take part in the one-day event, which consisted only of a running race. Some years later, more events were added to the Games to make them last for five days. These sports included the long jump, throwing the javelin and discus, chariot racing, boxing and wrestling. Another event was pankration, a mixture of boxing and wrestling. The event had no rules, except that biting or poking your opponent in the eye was not allowed!

An amphora vase depicting two athletes competing in pankration

The ruins of ancient Olympia

The early Olympic Games were a religious festival in honour of the god Zeus. People came from all over the Greek world to watch the Games and to take part. As the city-states were often at war, a month before the Games messengers were sent from the city-state of Elis, near Olympia, to announce the 'Olympic truce' for one month before the Games. This meant that people could travel to Olympia in safety. Everyone was allowed to watch the Games, except married women, and there was room for about 50 000 people in the stadium.

The events were judged by a *Hellanodikos*, or judge, and winners were adorned with a wreath made from olive leaves. After the Games, there was a feast. Oxen were barbecued, jugglers and acrobats performed, merchants did business and politicians made speeches.

ACTIVITIES

1. Answer the questions.
   a. When were the first Olympic Games held?
   b. Who took part in the first Games?
   c. Why were the Games held?
   d. Why was an Olympic truce necessary?
   e. Which group of people was not allowed to watch the Games?
   f. Who judged the event? What were the winners awarded with?
2. Think about what you have learnt in this unit. What type of people were not allowed to take part in the Games?
3. Find words in the text that mean the following:
   a. permitted
   b. applying force with your teeth
   c. pushing your finger (into something)
   d. a temporary suspension of fighting
   e. a ring of leaves
4. What Olympic events do you like best? In your opinion, are there any other sports or games that should be included in the modern Olympics?
5. Work in groups. Invent a new sport or game that you think should be included in the Olympics.

Work it out

CONCEPT MAP

Use the words in the word cloud to create your own unit map in your notebook. Write any connecting texts you need.

Hellenistic period Athens Hellenistic kingdoms **early civilisations**
Alexander the Great **Ancient Greece** Peloponnesian War
Greco-Persian Wars democracy diarchy Minoan culture
polis Sparta
Archaic period colonisation of the Mediterranean
Classical period tyranny
aristocracy Macedonia Mycenaean culture

SELF-ASSESSMENT

Carry out a self-assessment of what you have learnt in this unit. Choose one answer for each question and then check your answers.

1. The Minoan civilisation appeared in ...
   a. Crete.
   b. the Peloponnese.
   c. Mycenae.
2. Social conflict arose during the Archaic period because ...
   a. land was distributed unfairly.
   b. the peasants did not want to work the land.
   c. both a) and b).
3. In the Archaic period, what made merchants rich?
   a. Hellenisation
   b. Colonisation
   c. Tyranny
4. The Greeks beat the Persians at the battles of ...
   a. Athens and Corinth.
   b. Marathon and Sparta.
   c. Marathon and Salamis.
5. Which league did Athens lead?
   a. The League of Corinth
   b. The Delian League
   c. The Athenian League
6. In Classical Greece, laws were passed by ...
   a. the *Ecclesia*.
   b. the Acropolis.
   c. the *Boule*.
7. Which of the following people were citizens of Athens?
   a. Women born in Athens
   b. Free men from any Greek polis
   c. Free men born in Athens
8. In Sparta, which group of people did the hardest work?
   a. The Spartans
   b. The *helots*
   c. The *perioeci*
9. How long did it take Alexander the Great to build his empire?
   a. 13 years
   b. 12 years
   c. 11 years
10. What was the name of the kingdoms formed after Alexander the Great's death?
    a. The Greek kingdoms
    b. The Hellenistic kingdoms
    c. The Hellenisation kingdoms

02 Greek civilisation

<< LOOKING BACK

- What are the characteristics of a civilisation?
- What were Ancient Greek city-states called?
- How were Ancient Greek gods different from Ancient Egyptian gods?
- Which two Ancient Greek city-states were the most powerful?
- What was the purpose of the building shown in picture A?
- Identify the position in society of the man on the vase in picture C.

C **Pottery:** Athenian red-figure pottery, 5th century BC

B **Architecture:** The theatre at Delphi

A **Architecture:** The Parthenon in the Acropolis of Athens

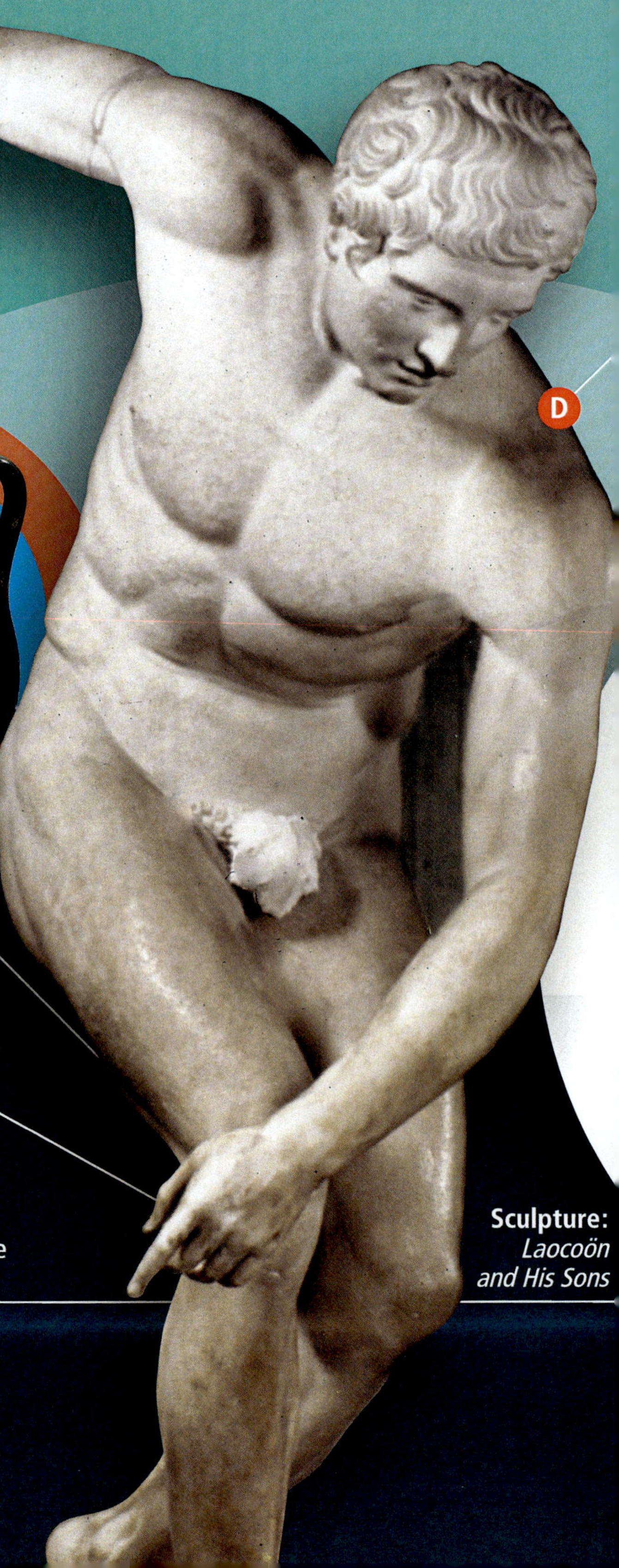

D **Sculpture:** *Laocoön and His Sons*

Sculpture:
A Roman copy of Myron's *Discobolus*

The missing marbles

In the early 19th century, a Scottish nobleman, the Earl of Elgin, became fascinated with the marble sculptures and inscriptions in the Parthenon temple in Athens.

Ancient Greek civilisation had ended more than 1 000 years before and the region was now controlled by the Ottoman Empire. However, Elgin, who was the British ambassador to the empire, managed to convince the Ottoman ruler, the sultan, to let him acquire the marbles and remove them from the Parthenon. Elgin took the marbles away over a 12-year period between 1801 and 1812. The British government then bought the marbles from Elgin in 1816. They were later given to the British Museum, where they are still on show today. For many years, Greece has demanded the return of the marbles, claiming that the sultan had no right to give away their artistic treasures and that they should be returned to their true home. The British argue that the marbles are best cared for in the museum and that they are conserving them as part of the world's shared heritage.

- Why do you think Greek art and architecture is considered to be so important?
- Where do you think the Elgin marbles should be kept: in Athens or in the British Museum in London?

LOOKING FORWARD >>

- What were Spartan slaves called?
- Can you name any Ancient Greek gods?
- What was an acropolis?
- What were Ancient Greek sculptures used for?
- What material was used to build the Parthenon?

1 Life in Ancient Greek city-states

1.1 The economy

The level of prosperity enjoyed by the Ancient Greeks was based on strong economic development. Their main economic activity was **arable farming**, with wheat, olives and grapes being the main crops. Other important economic activities were livestock farming and craftwork. They mainly crafted pottery, textiles and metal objects.

The goods produced from these economic activities were the basis of Ancient Greece's **trade**, which was a very important part of the economies of the city-states on the coast. The city-state of **Athens** had the **largest trade economy** in all of Greece thanks to their naval superiority and their leadership of the Delian League. The port of **Piraeus** was the centre of exportation of wine, olive oil, pottery and metal, and importation of wheat, wood and slaves.

1.2 Society

There were two main social groups in Ancient Greece: **free people** and **slaves**. Furthermore, free people were divided into two subgroups: **citizens** and **non-citizens**.

Society in Ancient Greece

Slaves

Slaves were not considered to be human beings. They were either the property of the state or of the wealthy. Slaves did the majority of the hard labour, such as mining, and domestic work in the homes of the wealthy. They were often prisoners of war or people who could not pay their **debts**. In Sparta, slaves were known as *helots*.

Free people

Non-citizens

Non-citizens did not have political rights and could not participate in the governance of the city-state. Women, foreigners and semi-free labourers were considered non-citizens.

Citizens

To be a citizen of a city-state, you had to be male and the son of a citizen. This meant only a minority of the population were citizens. Citizens in city-states had political rights and could take part in the governance of the city-state. They also had to pay taxes and do military service.

DAILY LIFE IN ATHENS

Athenian **men** spent most of their time doing business. In their free time, they would go to the baths and the gymnasium, as well as attending sporting and artistic events in honour of the gods.

What were Spartan slaves called?

ACTIVITIES

1. List the main crops farmed by the Ancient Greeks.
2. Which city-state had the largest trade economy?
3. List some tasks performed by slaves in Ancient Greece.
4. Find out what a *symposium* was. Where did they take place?
5. In pairs, choose one of the social groups from Ancient Greece – e.g. slaves, citizens and non-citizens – and prepare a wall display about their daily life.

2 Greek culture

Can you name any Ancient Greek gods?

The Ancient Greeks lived in various independent city-states, but they identified themselves as a group because of their culture, i.e. their language, religion, philosophy and art. The main characteristics of Ancient Greek culture were:

- **Anthropocentrism**: the Greeks believed human beings were the most important entities on Earth. They had an anthropocentric view on life.
- **Rationalism**: they also thought in a rational way. They reflected on human reality, carried out research and proposed hypotheses, which they then tried to prove.
- **Beauty**: they aimed to achieve beauty in their art and architecture.
- **Education**: they educated people to have a strong sense of civic duty.

DID YOU KNOW?

Greek women used powdered chalk and white lead as make-up on their faces. This was to make their skin look pale, a sign of beauty in Ancient Greece. The problem was that white lead was poisonous! The word *cosmetics* comes from the Greek *kosmetikos*, meaning 'harmony and order'.

Has make-up evolved much since then?

2.1 Literature

The Greeks were responsible for the creation of several **literary genres**: epic poetry, lyric poetry and theatre.

Epic poems were very long. They narrated events in the lives of epic heroes or events in the history of a culture or civilisation.

The most important writer of epic poetry was **Homer**. Homer's greatest works were ***The Iliad***, which recounts an episode from the Trojan War, and ***The Odyssey***, which tells of the adventures of Odysseus on his return from Troy.

Another important genre was **lyric poetry**, the subject of which was the poet's feelings. This type of poetry was accompanied by a string instrument called the lyre.

The Greeks also created the **theatre**. Plays were acted out in theatres. The most well-known genres of theatre were tragedies and comedies.

- **Tragedies** were about kings, heroes and gods who decided people's fate. The most important authors of tragedies were Aeschylus, Sophocles and Euripides.
- **Comedies** were about everyday people and involved a lot of social and political commentary. Aristophanes was the most important author of comedies.

ODYSSEUS AND THE SIRENS' SONG

"First you will come to the Sirens, who enchant all men who come near them. If anyone unsuspecting approaches and hears their singing, his wife and children will never welcome him home again, for they will charm him with the sweetness of their song. On the beach before the meadow where they live, there is a great pile of dead men's bones with the flesh still rotting off them."

HOMER, *The Odyssey* (adapted)

ACTIVITIES

6. In Ancient Greece, was identity more related to culture or geography? Explain your answer.
7. Explain the difference between a tragedy and a comedy.
8. Read the extract from Homer's *The Odyssey* in the box above. Find out who or what sirens were in Ancient Greek literature. Then, read the text again and say why there were bones on the beach.

2.2 Philosophy and science

Ancient Greece is considered to be the birthplace of **philosophy** and science, which originated in the city-states of Ionia during the 6th century BC. Here, philosophers and experts in science looked for explanations for the origin and nature of the Universe. **Pythagoras**, a very important mathematician, was one of these figures.

Later, in Classical and Hellenistic Greece, philosophers focused on human beings and society. In Athens, there were three great philosophers who were extremely influential: **Socrates**, **Plato** and **Aristotle**.

2.3 Greek religion

The Greeks were **polytheists**, meaning they worshipped more than one god. The gods were **anthropomorphic**, which means they looked and acted like humans, but, at the same time, were immortal.

THE GREEK GODS

According to Greek religion, the gods lived on Mount Olympus. The most important god was Zeus, the god of thunder and son of Cronus, the god of time. Zeus shared control of the world between himself and his brothers.

Although he was married to Hera, Zeus had children by other goddesses. He also had children by mortal women and these children were **demigods** or heroes. The most famous child was Heracles, also known as Hercules. There were also other minor gods and goddesses, such as the Muses, who were the goddeses of the arts and sciences.

1. Zeus (god of gods); **2.** Hera (family); **3.** Athena (home); **4.** Apollo (beauty); **5.** Demeter (harvest); **6.** Poseidon (sea); **7.** Aphrodite (love); **8.** Artemis (hunting); **9.** Ares (war); **10.** Dionysus (wine); **11.** Hephaestus (blacksmiths); **12.** Hades (underworld); **13.** Hermes (messenger god)

Religion in Ancient Greece came from a need to answer questions which were common to other religions, such as what is the origin of the world and human beings. However, in Greek religion there were no obligations apart from sacrificing animals in honour of the gods and holding festivals.

Some aspects of Greek religion and religious sites were **pan-Hellenic**, which means they were of importance throughout the Greek world. This was the case with the **Oracle of Delphi**, which was a place where visitors asked the god Apollo to help them make decisions.

BIG THINKER

Socrates was born in Athens in 469 BC. He came from a humble family, but when he reached middle age he began asking himself deep philosophical questions about the world around him. A group of young men began to follow his rational way of thinking, but his ideas threatened to upset the Athenian authorities.

He was eventually put on trial and **sentenced** to death by drinking a cup of hemlock (a poisonous plant), which he drank himself.

Why would he do such a thing?

THE OLYMPIC GAMES

As a way of honouring their gods, the Ancient Greeks held **games**, which consisted of various physical and sporting competitions, such as racing and wrestling. The different city-states would send their best athletes to compete.

The most important games were held every four years in honour of Zeus. They took place at the shrine at Olympia, from which they get their name, the **Olympic Games**. Only Greeks participated in the Olympic Games. Throughout the duration of the Games, there was a general **truce** between feuding city-states.

ACTIVITIES

9. Find out what Plato's relationship to Socrates was, and what Aristotle's relationship to Alexander the Great was. You can use the internet or reference books to help you.

10. Name a religious site that was considered pan-Hellenic.

11. How do the Greek gods differ from Egyptian gods in terms of appearance?

3 Greek architecture

What was an acropolis?

3.1 Characteristics of Greek architecture

The fundamental principle of Ancient Greek architecture was the quest **for beauty**. For the Ancient Greeks, beauty consisted of proportion, balance, serenity, accurate measurements and harmony. The fundamental aim of Ancient Greek architecture was that citizens would enjoy looking at it.

Greek architecture was made for **people**. The buildings were designed for civil life and they were not as large as those of the ancient civilisations of Egypt and Mesopotamia.

The Greeks built with stone, constructing buildings with architraves supported by columns. They did not use arches or vaults. These buildings were built to a certain standard, or **order**, which determined how they were constructed and decorated. There were three main architectural orders: Ionic, Doric and Corinthian.

GREEK ARCHITECTURAL ORDERS

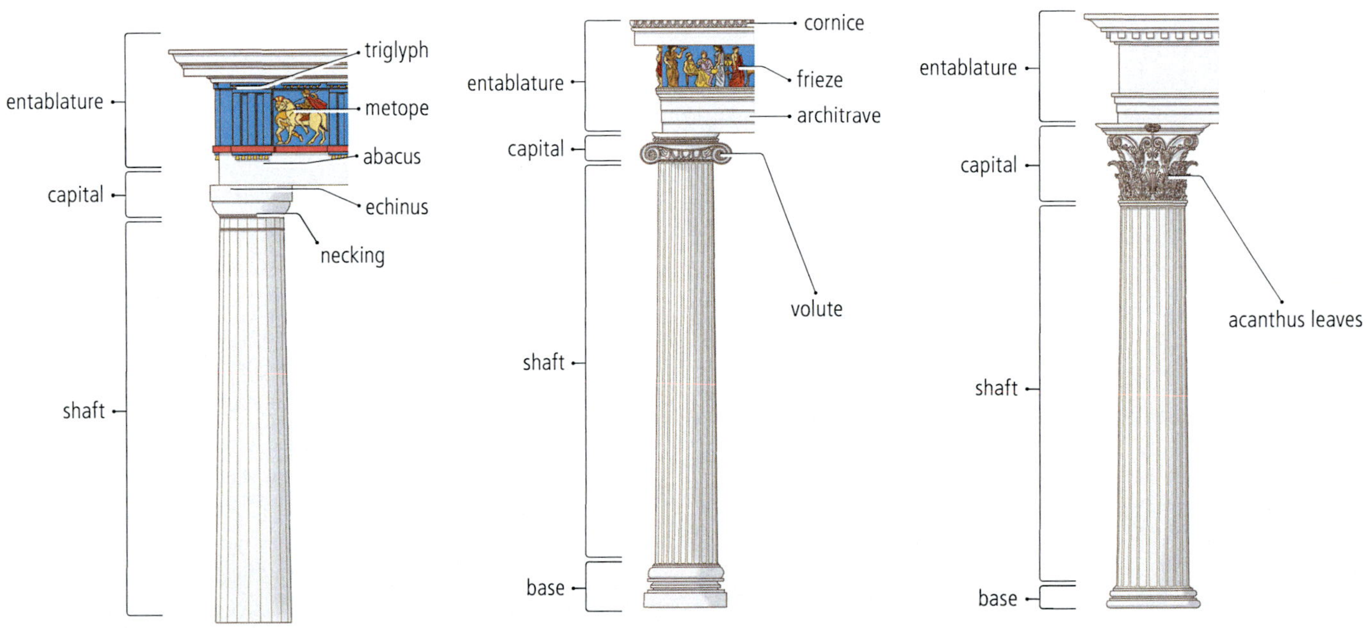

Doric order: This was the oldest order. The column had no base, the shaft was thick and **fluted**, and the capital was made up of three rectilinear pieces: the abacus, echinus and necking.

In the entablature, the most important element was the frieze, divided into triglyphs (three vertical bands) and flat sections called metopes, where **bas-reliefs** were usually carved.

Ionic order: These structures were lighter. The column had a base and was slender, with a narrow shaft and grooves. The capital was made up of spirals known as volutes.

The entablature was divided into two sections: architrave and frieze. The frieze was not divided up.

Corinthian order: This order was the most common during the Hellenistic period and extremely influential after that. It had similar characteristics to the Ionic order, but the capital was different: it was made up of a basket from which acanthus leaves emerged.

3.2 Important buildings

THEATRES

Theatres were usually built on hillsides, using the differences in height to create rows or seats. They had excellent acoustics.

Theatres had different areas which served a variety of purposes:

- a **seating area** for the audience
- a circular **orchestra** where the **chorus** was located
- a stage, or **proscenium**, which was reserved for the actors

The theatre at Epidaurus

TEMPLES

Temples were designed to house the statue of a god. In general, only priests could enter a temple, so religious celebrations were held outside. The buildings were intended to be viewed from the outside, so great care was taken with their proportions.

Temples often formed parts of large religious sites called **sanctuaries**. These sites were located in magnificent locations of natural beauty and housed temples, theatres, stadiums and other buildings. The most important temples were the temple to Zeus at Olympia, the temple to Apollo at Delphi, and the Parthenon in Athens, which honoured Athena, the **patron** of Athens.

The Parthenon

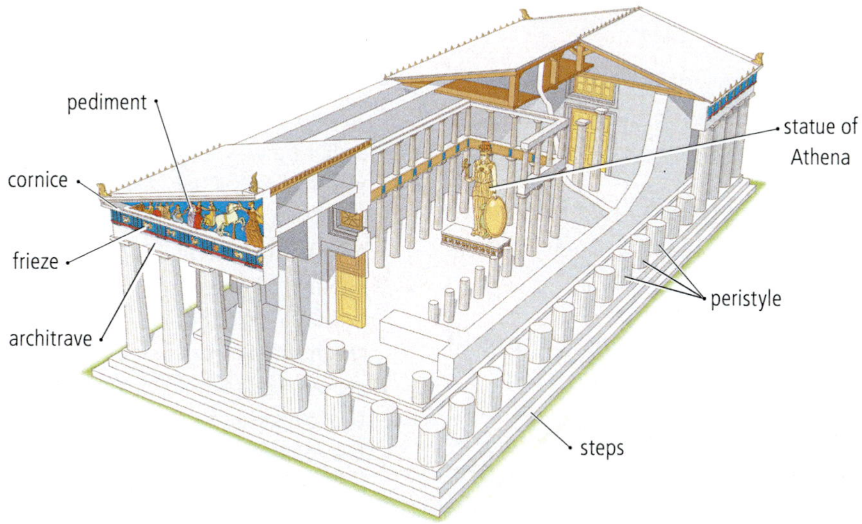

DID YOU KNOW?

The Greek theatre of Epidaurus has incredible acoustics. A performer standing on the stage can be heard in the back rows of the seating area, some 60 metres away! The theatre was discovered in 1881, under a layer of earth.

How do we hear actors on stage nowadays?

The Temple of Concordia was built in the Doric order.

ACTIVITIES

12. How was beauty expressed in Greek architecture? For what purpose did the Greeks construct their buildings?
13. Draw a Greek theatre in your notebook and label each of its parts, explaining their function and who used them.
14. Copy the drawings of the columns and entablatures from the three orders in your notebook and label the different parts.

4 Greek pottery and sculpture

What were Ancient Greek sculptures used for?

4.1 Pottery

Very few Ancient Greek paintings have survived the test of time. However, a lot of pottery has survived and gives us a good idea of the style the Greeks drew in and how they used colour.

- **Geometric pottery**: Early pottery decoration was geometric. This style was most common between the 11th and 8th centuries BC.
- **Black-figure pottery**: Between the 7th and 5th centuries BC, they began to incorporate human figures in black on a red background.
- **Red-figure pottery**: Beginning in the 5th century BC, they depicted humans in red on a black background.

Geometric pottery from the 8th century BC

Black-figure pottery from the 6th century BC

Red-figure pottery from the 5th–4th century BC

4.2 Sculpture

Sculpture was one of the most important art forms in Ancient Greece. Sculptures were used to adorn temples, depict gods, immortalise athletes and to remember the dead.

The most common subject was the **human figure**. The Greeks tried to achieve beauty through perfect forms, harmonious proportions and balance. Their subjects were always beautiful, with perfect bodies, muscles and faces.

To achieve balance and accurate proportions, Greek sculptors created **canons of proportions**. These canons evolved over time.

Greek sculptors used marble and bronze as **materials** for their sculptures. It is possible to identify **three phases of Greek sculpture**: Archaic, Classical and Hellenistic.

CANON OF PROPORTIONS

A canon was a model of beauty which a sculpture was supposed to match. The sculptor Polyclitus devised a canon in which the body should be seven times the height of the head. We can see an example of this in his sculpture *Doryphoros*.

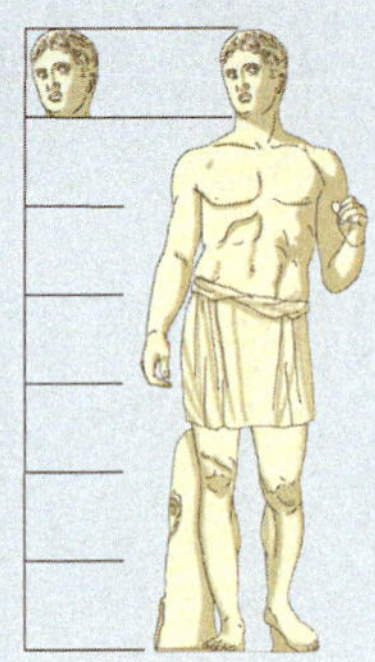

ACTIVITIES

15. What was the most common subject of Ancient Greek sculpture?
16. Create a timeline showing the evolution of Greek pottery. Write the main characteristics of each period below the timeline.
17. Look at the red and black-figure vases above. Try to describe what is depicted on each one.
18. Find out how the sculptor Lysippus changed Polyclitus' canon of proportions.

Archaic sculpture

Archaic sculpture emerged in the 7th century BC. It was strongly influenced by Egyptian sculpture. As a result of this influence, Archaic sculpture had the following characteristics:

- Figures were usually **front-facing**.
- Their bodies were **rigid** and **lacked expression**.

However, the style of sculpture gradually evolved over the course of the 6th century BC:

- **Expressive features**, such as smiling, were introduced.
- More **detailed modelling** of the muscles and hair were also introduced.

The most common subjects of Archaic sculpture were **kouroi** and **korai**.

KOUROI

Kouroi were sculptures of male youths, used as memorials in the tombs of young warriors. The kouroi were depicted naked, with one foot slightly forward, their arms held next to their body, a slight smile and long hair.

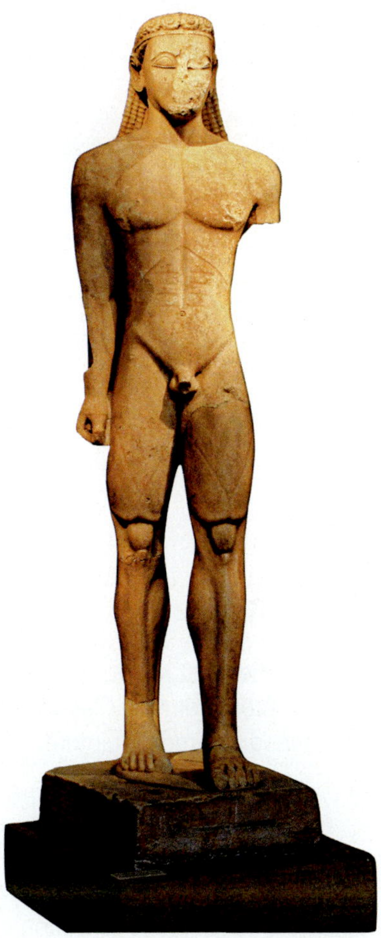

Kouros from Sounion, from about 600 BC

KORAI

Korai were sculptures of young girls. These were the female equivalent of the kouroi, but unlike the kouroi, they were always depicted dressed and their arms were not always by their side.

Kore no. 670 from the Acropolis of Athens, from around 510 BC

DID YOU KNOW?

Kouroi and korai were sometimes painted. However, over time, the paint wore away. Some examples of painted sculptures have survived, such as the one below, discovered in the Greek island of Chios. It dates from around 520 BC.

Which other ancient civilisation painted its sculptures?

ACTIVITIES

19. What were the most common subjects of Archaic sculpture?

20. How did the style of Archaic sculpture evolve between the 7th and 6th centuries?

21. Find out information about the korai of the Acropolis of Athens. When were they discovered? What happened to them?

Classical sculpture

The Classical period of Greek history covered the **5th and 4th centuries BC**. The most important sculptors of the 5th century BC were Polyclitus, Myron and Phidias. **Polyclitus** was the sculptor of the *Diadumenos* and the *Doryphoros*, two of the most famous sculptures of the Classical period. **Myron** sculpted the famous *Discobolus*. **Phidias** sculpted the reliefs on the Parthenon in the Acropolis of Athens.

The work of these three sculptors shares the following characteristics:

- **Proportion** was of great importance. This is evident in Polyclitus' creation of a canon of proportions.
- The figures were **expressive**. This was achieved without using forced gestures, as the sculptor wanted the figures to look natural.
- The figures were not simply front-facing: they were intended to be seen from **several angles**.
- The swinging of the legs, arms and hips gave the figures **movement**, without exaggerating their positions.
- The use of **balance** when depicting movement and expression conveyed serenity.

In the 4th century BC, sculptors such as Lysippus and Praxiteles began to create more dynamic sculptures. As the 4th century BC progressed, Classical sculpture became more slender with the adoption of Praxiteles' canon. His canon stipulated that the height of the figure should be seven and a half times the height of the head.

Myron's *Discobolus* depicts the movement of an athlete building up momentum to throw a discus.

In *Hermes and the Infant Dionysus*, Praxiteles represents the interaction of two figures through facial expressions.

NIKE TYING A SANDAL

Although there were sculptures of female nudes during the Classical period, it was more common for figures of women, which always represented goddesses, to be covered. However, the 'wet **drapery**' technique made it possible to make out their figure, such as in this relief of Nike, the goddess of victory, adjusting her sandal.

ACTIVITIES

22. List the most important sculptors from the Classical period of Greek sculpture.

23. List five characteristics of Classical sculpture from the 5th century BC.

24. How does Praxiteles' canon of proportions differ from that of Polyclitus? Turn to page 30 to help you compare.

Hellenistic sculpture

As a result of territorial expansion into the East during the 3rd century BC, Greek sculptors became **influenced by Eastern art.** This influence considerably changed the style of Classical sculpture, marking the transition to Hellenistic sculpture.

The main characteristics of Hellenistic sculpture were:

- Sculptors created **more personal pieces of work**, which were defined by their own individual **tastes**.
- This period featured greater **realism** and **naturalism**.
- Classical beauty, conceived as harmony and serenity, gave way to **dramatic tension** and **exaggerated movements.**
- **New subjects**, which had previously been inconceivable, began to appear, such as the elderly, children and the dying.

The sculpture *Laocoön and His Sons* is the finest example of Hellenistic sculpture.

This relief from the Pergamon Altar commemorates a military victory.

Victory of Samothrace by Paeonius. This sculpture represents a goddess on the **prow** of a ship.

ACTIVITIES

25. How did Greek colonisation influence the style of sculpture in the 3rd century BC?

26. List four main characteristics of Hellenistic sculpture.

27. Get into four groups and create a group slideshow presentation. Each group chooses one of the following topics:

- Archaic sculpture
- Classical sculpture
- Hellenistic sculpture
- Greek pottery

Each group member researches one work of sculpture or pottery and prepares a slide. Include an image of the work and label it. Then, put all the slides together and give your presentation as a group.

Discovery techniques

ANALYSING WORKS OF ARCHITECTURE

Classical Greek culture is considered to be the foundation of Western culture. Greek culture, especially philosophy, greatly influenced the Roman Empire. From here, Ancient Greek ideas spread throughout Europe and to much of the **Western world**. Today we live in democratic societies, but we can also see the influence of Greek architecture all around us.

When we analyse a work of architecture, we need to include information about various aspects of the work: the technical complexity of the work, its location, its aesthetics and its function. To do this, you need to follow the steps described below. Let's take the example of the Parthenon to take us through the steps:

1. Background

Find out information that can help you put the work into context:

- The **type of building** it is: religious (e.g. a temple), institutional (e.g. a palace), private (e.g. a home) or public (e.g. a theatre).
- **Where and when** it was built.
- The **architect**, unless the architect is anonymous.
- The person who **ordered its construction**.

Type of building	Religious. It is a temple dedicated to the goddess Athena Parthenos.
Location	Athens
Year or period of construction	5th century BC
Architects	Ictinus and Callicrates
Who ordered its construction?	Pericles, an Athenian magistrate

2. Commentary

Carry out an analysis of the technical aspects of the work. Include information on the following:

- The **construction material** used (e.g. granite, marble, limestone, sandstone, etc.)
- The **structural elements** (e.g. columns, walls, roof, steps, etc.)
- The building's **floor plan** (i.e. the shape of the floor – square, rectangular, oval, etc.)
- The **style of architecture**

Construction material	Marble
Description of the structural elements	It is built on a set of steps. The columns form a peristyle, and the walls support an architrave structure and a **gable** roof.
Description of the building's floor plan	The temple has a rectangular floor plan.
Description of the style	The building was built according to the Doric order.

What material was used to build the Parthenon?

To illustrate the information you provide, you can label a photograph of the structure and draw its floor plan.

The capitals are made up of a necking, abacus and echinus.

In the entablature we can see the architrave, the frieze – divided into triglyphs and metopes – and the cornice.

The columns have no base and the shaft is fluted.

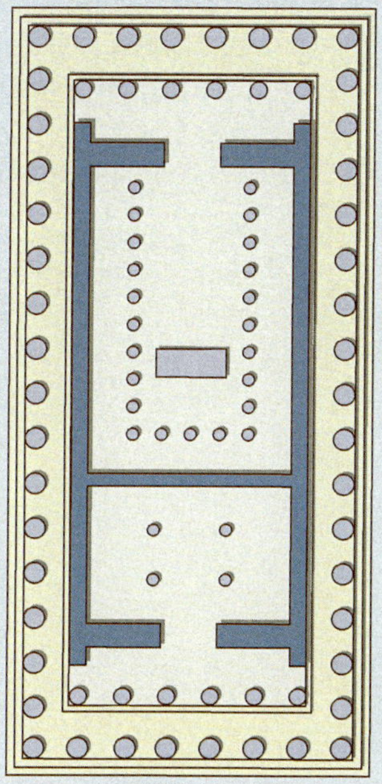

A floor plan of the Parthenon

3. Conclusion

In this last part of our commentary, we should evaluate the impact of the building and describe its function.

The Parthenon had a religious function, as it was a temple dedicated to the goddess Athena and it was built within the sanctuary of the Acropolis of Athens. It also had an aesthetic function: the building follows the principles of proportion and the metopes and pediments are decorated with sculptures.

In addition to being religious, it had a political purpose: Pericles wanted the temple to show the prestige of Athens. Despite the fact that the Parthenon has suffered some damage, it is still one of the greatest examples of architecture in the world.

ACTIVITIES

1. Find a building in your local area or somewhere in your autonomous community that has been influenced by Greek architecture. Take a picture of it or look for one online. With a classmate, analyse the building, following the steps above. Include background, a commentary and a conclusion.
2. Write an analysis of the Temple of Athena Nike at the Acropolis of Athens, shown in the photo on the right. To help you, use the information in this book, carry out research online and consult art history books and encyclopaedias.

The Temple of Athena Nike at the Acropolis of Athens

Revision activities

1. List the main economic activities of Ancient Greece. Also, mention the products produced from these activities.

2. Explain how trade and economic prosperity were related in Ancient Greek city-states. Why was the city-state of Athens particularly prosperous?

3. Copy and complete the following diagram:

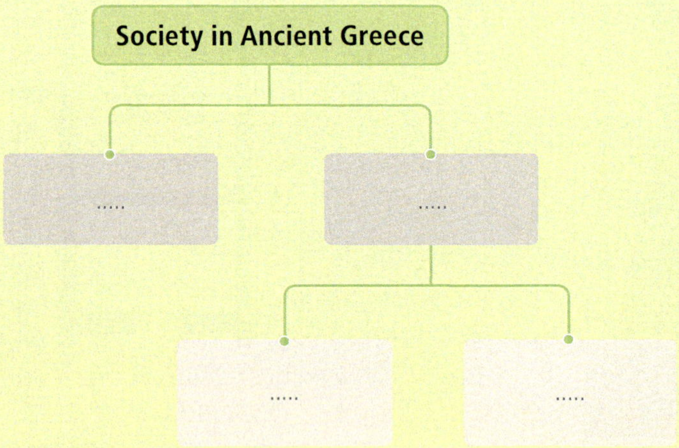

   a. Who were considered citizens in Ancient Greece? What were their rights and obligations?
   b. Who were considered to be non-citizens? Compare them to citizens.
   c. What status did slaves have in Ancient Greece? How did many of them become slaves? Do you think that they were treated as human beings?

4. Read the text below and answer the questions that follow:

> “That some people rule and others are ruled is something not only necessary, but appropriate, because from the hour of their birth, some people are destined to be ruled and others to rule [...] He, who can more or less understand rational thought, but is not capable of thinking rationally by himself, is a slave by nature [...] It is clear that some men are by nature free and that others are slaves, and that for them slavery is both appropriate and correct.”
>
> Aristotle, *Politics* (adapted)

   a. Identify the two main concepts of the text.
   b. What period of Ancient Greek history do you think the text is from?
   c. What do you know about the author of the text, Aristotle?
   d. Explain what type of text it is (e.g. religious, philosophical, political, etc.).

5. Write definitions for the following terms: *anthropocentrism, tragedy, comedy, philosophy, epic poetry, lyric poetry.*

6. Make sentences using all the words in each group:
   a. Parthenon; Pericles; Athena; Acropolis
   b. language; religion; independent city-states; anthropocentric; identified as a group
   c. anthropomorphic; polytheists; humans; immortal
   d. Pan-Hellenic; cults; Greek world; followed; throughout

7. Find out the origin of the word *philosophy*. Use a dictionary or the internet to help you.

8. Homer is considered to be the greatest writer of epic poetry in Ancient Greece. His two greatest works were *The Odyssey* and *The Iliad*. Choose one of these two works and find information online to complete the table below in your notebook:

Type of literary work	.....
Central character	.....
Setting (during or after the Trojan War)	.....
Events that take place	.....

9. Classical Greek architecture was one of the main inspirations for Neoclassical architecture, a movement which began in the mid-18th century. Elements of Greek architecture can be seen in cities all over the world. If you live in a city, look out for a building that has elements of Greek architecture. Take a picture of it and prepare an analysis to present in class.

10. Identify the periods these works of pottery belong to. Justify your answers.

11 Match the terms with their definitions. Then write full sentences in your notebook.

a. comedy
b. order
c. Homer
d. tragedy
e. canon
f. anthropocentrism
g. sanctuaries
h. architectural beauty

1. A standard to which Ancient Greek temples were built. There were three: Ionic, Doric and Corinthian.
2. A culture where human beings were their main focus.
3. The most important writer of epic poetry.
4. A play which featured everyday people.
5. Proportion, balance, serenity, accurate measurements and harmony.
6. Large religious sites located in magnificent natural sites, which housed temples, theatres, stadiums and other buildings.
7. A play which featured kings, heroes and gods.
8. A model of beauty which a sculpture was supposed to match.

12 Compare these two sculptures. Write any similarities and differences you identify in your notebook.

This vocabulary may help you: *standing, male, nude, inspired by, rigid pose, no expression, slight movement.*

A

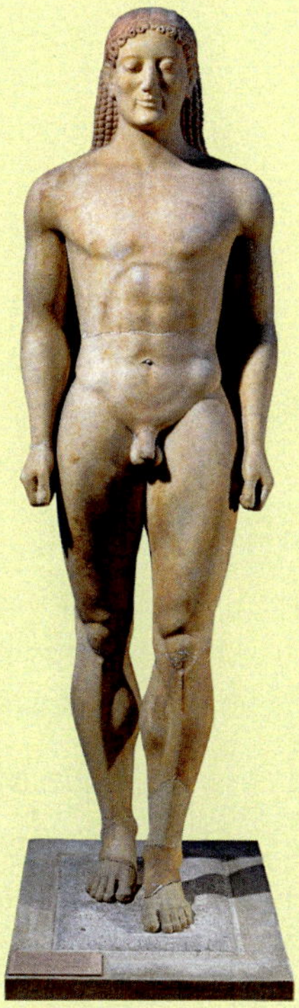

B

13 Study these two examples of Ancient Greek sculpture and fill in the table below.

A

B

Period	.....
Subject	.....
Facial expression	.....
Realism	.....
Other characteristics (proportion, movement, tension, angle, etc.)	.....

14 What is the odd one out? Write the three associated words in your notebook and explain how they are related to each other.

A
Polyclitus
Praxiteles
Myron
Phidias

B
Plato
Socrates
Pericles
Aristotle

C
Ionic
Doric
pottery
Corinthian

D
pediment
kore
frieze
architrave

Read and think

EDUCATION IN ANCIENT GREECE

Greek children were educated in different ways depending on where they lived. Education differed greatly between Athens and Sparta.

In ancient **Athens**, the purpose of education was to train boys to take part in public life and to prepare them for times of both peace and war. Only middle-class and upper-class boys went to school because schools cost money. They started school at the age of seven. The length of their education depended on their parents' wealth.

Schools were small, with only one teacher for every 10 to 20 boys. Pupils learnt reading, writing, simple mathematics and any other subjects the teacher decided were appropriate. Although they had wax-covered boards and a stylus to write with, they learnt most things off by heart. Athenian boys memorised epic poetry and learnt to play the lyre. In the afternoons they attended wrestling schools, where they took part in different sports.

Ancient Greek wrestlers

At the age of fourteen, tradesmen's children began to learn a trade, while the richer boys continued studying for four more years. When they were eighteen, they went to military school for two years. Rich Athenian girls learnt to read and write at home. They also learnt how to run a home and look after a family.

In ancient **Sparta**, the purpose of education was to produce good soldiers. Spartans believed in a life of discipline, self-sacrifice and simplicity. Spartan boys were sent to military school at the age of six or seven. They lived, trained and slept there. They were taught survival skills and other skills needed to be a great soldier. Although students were taught to read and write, this was not a priority for the ancient Spartans. Girls also went to school at the age of six or seven. They lived, slept and trained there too. They were taught wrestling, gymnastics, and combat skills. The Spartans believed that strong young women would produce strong babies.

Before you read the text, try to answer these questions:

a. Which Athenian children do you think went school?
b. What were they taught there?
c. Which Spartan children do you think went to school?
d. What were they taught there?

ACTIVITIES

1. Check your answers to the questions in the box above.
2. True or false? Correct the false statements.
   a. In Athens, all the boys went to school for the same amount of time.
   b. Athenian schoolboys learnt to play a musical instrument.
   c. They only learnt how to wrestle at wrestling schools.
   d. The Spartans believed that reading and writing were the most important skills to learn.
3. Work in pairs. Discuss these questions:
   What skills did the Greeks use in the Archaic period to colonise different places around the Mediterranean? Would any other skills have been useful to them?
4. Work in groups. Discuss and answer the questions.
   a. In your opinion, what is the purpose of education today?
   b. What specific skills would you teach someone who would like to be a: taxi driver, politician, teacher, shopkeeper?

Work it out

CONCEPT MAP

Use the words in the word cloud to create your own unit map in your notebook. Write any connecting texts you need.

Archaic · Ionic · free people · Plato · **architecture** · **economy** · orders · citizens · **Greek culture** · Socrates · **society** · **religion** · trade · lyric poetry · Classical · literary genres · Hellenistic · non-citizens · Doric · **sculpture** · slaves · **life in Ancient Greece** · theatre · Pythagoras · rationalism · Corinthian · arable farming · **philosophy and science** · **literature** · Aristotle · epic poetry

SELF-ASSESSMENT

Carry out a self-assessment of what you have learnt in this unit. Choose one answer for each question and then check your answers.

1. What was the main economic activity in Ancient Greece?
   a. Livestock farming
   b. Arable farming
   c. Craftwork

2. In Ancient Greece, women and foreigners were considered to be ...
   a. slaves.
   b. citizens.
   c. non-citizens.

3. The port of Piraeus was located in ...
   a. Sparta.
   b. Athens.
   c. Thebes.

4. Anthropocentric means ...
   a. centred on human beings.
   b. giving human characteristics to inanimate objects.
   c. dealing with the history of humanity.

5. The Ancient Greeks were ...
   a. atheists.
   b. monotheists.
   c. polytheists.

6. The Greek gods lived ...
   a. on Mount Olympus.
   b. in Delphi.
   c. in the Acropolis of Athens.

7. The Greeks built with ...
   a. stone.
   b. brick.
   c. wood.

8. The most common subject of Greek sculpture was ...
   a. animals.
   b. battles.
   c. people.

9. In Archaic sculpture, funerary statues of girls were called ...
   a. canons.
   b. kouroi.
   c. korai.

10. The most realistic Greek sculptures were made in the ...
    a. Archaic period.
    b. Classical period.
    c. Hellenistic period.

Big thinkers

Name: Cleisthenes
Lived: *c.*570–508 BC
Nationality: Athenian (Greek)
Interests: Politics

Bright ideas: Historians consider him 'the father of Athenian democracy'. He passed reforms to change Athens' voting system so that poor citizens could have an equal say in government. He also reduced the power of the aristocratic families by introducing the practice of 'ostracism'.

Name: Socrates
Lived: *c.*469–399 BC
Nationality: Athenian (Greek)
Interests: Ancient philosophy, epistemology, ethics

Bright ideas: Together with Plato and Aristotle, people consider him 'the father of Western philosophy'. A method of enquiry was named after him – the Socratic method – in which questioning and debate encourage critical thinking.

Glossary

Achievement (n): something done well or successfully through determination and hard work

Antiquity (n): another term for Ancient History

Arable (adj): good for growing crops

Aristocracy (n): the highest class in certain societies, typically made up of people born into wealthy families

Banish (v): to officially send someone away from a country or place as a punishment

Bas-relief (n): a relief sculpture in which the shapes stick out slightly from their background

Characterise (v): to describe the most obvious or typical qualities and features of somebody or something

Chorus (n): CLASSICAL THEATRE a group of performers who comment together on the action of a play

Court (n): the group made up of a king or queen, and his or her family, advisors, servants, etc.

Debt (n): a sum of money that a person or organisation owes

Demigod (n): a god of less importance than other gods; a human being who is worshipped as a god

Drapery (n): cloth, or something made from cloth; clothing that hangs loosely in folds

Draw lots (v): to make a decision at random by choosing from a group of objects, for example pieces of paper or sticks, that are all the same except for one

Egalitarian (adj): believing that all people are equal and deserve equal rights and opportunities

Enslave (v): to cause someone to lose their freedom; to make someone a slave

Fate (n): the things that happen to someone; destiny

Fluted (adj): with a pattern of curves cut around the outside

Gable (n): the top end of a wall of a building, just below the roof, that is shaped like a triangle

Harsh (adj): difficult to live in due to unpleasant or dangerous conditions

Hegemony (n): dominance by one state or social group over others

League (n): POLITICS an association or group of people, organisations or countries that come together because they have similar objectives or interests

Overtake (v): to become more successful or better than something or someone else

Overthrow (v): to remove a ruler or government from power by force

Patron (n): a person or god who is a special guardian, protector or supporter

Philosophy (n): the study of ideas about the meaning of life

Prow (n): the front part of a boat or a ship

Quarters (n): rooms or buildings used to live or sleep in, especially by military personnel

Quest (n): a long and difficult search for something

Sentence (v): to give a punishment to someone who has committed a crime or an offence

Settlement (n): a previously uninhabited place where people establish a community

Standard of living (n): the amount of money and level of comfort that a particular person or group has

Subject matter (n): the things that are shown in a work of art or discussed in a debate

Taste (n): the particular things a person likes, for example in music or art

Truce (n): an agreement between the parties involved in a war or battle to temporarily stop fighting

Wear away (v): to erode or disappear

Western world (n): a term which refers to Western European countries and countries in North and South America which have been influenced by Spanish, Portuguese, French and British colonisation (other countries, such as Australia and New Zealand, are also included)